THE WHITE EYELASH

ALSO BY SUSAN KINSOLVING

Dailies & Rushes

Among Flowers
in collaboration with artist Susan Colgan

THE WHITE EYELASH

BY SUSAN KINSOLVING

GROVE PRESS
NEW YORK

Published simultaneously in Canada
Printed in the United States of America

FIRST EDITION

Library of Congress Cataloging-in-Publication Data

Kinsolving, Susan.
      The white eyelash / by Susan Kinsolving.
      p. cm.
      ISBN 0-8021-4029-7
      I. Title.

  PS3561.I578W47 2003
  813'.54—dc21   2003049073

Grove Press
841 Broadway
New York, NY 10003

03 04 05 06 07   10 9 8 7 6 5 4 3 2 1

Acknowledgments

My thanks to the editors of the following magazines
and anthologies in which some of these poems previously
appeared:

Connecticut Review
For a Living, University of Illinois Press
Kaleidoscope
Ontario Review
The Paris Review
Poetry
Shenandoah
Snakes: An Anthology of Serpent Tales
Solo
Southwest Review
Yale Review

I appreciate the encouragement and support given to me by:

Foundation Ledig-Rowohlt, Switzerland
Carol Franc Buck Foundation, Nevada
Chautauqua Institute, New York
Dunvegan Castle Festival, Scotland
Faith Middleton, Connecticut Public Radio
Glimmerglass Opera, New York
The International Festival of Arts & Ideas, Connecticut
The Geraldine R. Dodge Poetry Festival, New Jersey
The Sunken Garden Poetry Festival, Connecticut
The Robinson Jeffers Tor House Foundation, California

To Richard Howard, man of letters, mentor, and marvel,
again and always, my gratitude.

Contents

For Caroline and Eliza

BLURRING MYSELF

SOME SNOWS

Some snows are soulful, slow cello sounds
settling the world into a serene sleep.
Others are fast, feathery, flutes unfaltering,

puffing the landscape into airy upholstered
shapes. But last night under the porch
floodlight, the flakes zigzagged, whirled

into a concerted chaos, and I stood there
with that great glad expansiveness so seldom
had. Any winter could be my last, yours,

ours. How dreadful the knowing and not
knowing. How alive the alchemy of snow,
the wonder of winter falling through

the dead of night, veiling and shrouding
our dark world white. Arms outstretched,
I circled, cold, spinning my symphony

in the flurry. White-haired, I was without
a worry, unimaginably free, revolving,
laughing, lavish, blurring myself from me.

INKLING

The mind of the mountaineer floats on the lull
of low tide, a speck of salt in one eye, a grain
of sand in the other. The surgeon drifts and grips
the worn handles of an old plow, pushing that
image deep into furrows, unearthing grubs, worms,

stones. While the pilot's windshield shows
a silent movie of tap dancers shaking tambourines,
the artist's canvas turns into a telescope, and
galaxies appear. But it is the child who comes
closest to being a tree or turtle or another

of some other kind. Only imagination lets us
glimpse around the corners of our fate, the way
our dreams take us where our travels never do.
Ah, other worlds, other lives, what is not
true, kaleidoscope turning, changing points of view.

THIN BLOOD
Aka *idiopathic thrombocytopenia purpura*

First bruises, plums on the thighs, soon
another attack, blackberries on the back. Then
steroids are started for a round-the-clock thrill
until a crash comes and the bruises are done.
On to acne and a face ballooning with hair.
Next dare: a nice Shakespearean sacrifice,
a surgically removed spleen. (What could it mean?
On Saint Valentine's! Be mine.) Eyes go bright blood red.
Other patients are dead. So when both ankles break:
piece o' cake. With this new year, who's not without
fear, but damn happy, even grateful, just to be here?

CARPE NOCTEM

Too often, getting a grip is the gauge,
the old having a handle on things
as if they came with a handle, like
a pitcher, a drawer. And even then
there's a spill, a real mess of what-

not and what-have-you. So I lie still
and rely on the night nurse to raise
the side rails (not exactly against
my will). Then I curl my hands over
the cool aluminum tubes. This grasp

on life is true. Ask the ones
in prison or the zoo. Don't fly
off the handle, they'll tell you.
Surrender can be sweet. Pill or
liquid, raise the bars and . . . sleep.

29,000 BATHTUB TOYS
After an article in *The National Geographic*

A storm just south of the Aleutian Islands,
one cargo container slips off, breaks. All
its yellow ducks, green frogs, red beavers,
and blue turtles drift in the counterclock-
wise tides of the Northern Pacific. Ice traps
some; others wash up, bouncing onto beaches
by the Bering Sea. After surgery, wreckage
as whimsy amuses me, polar extremes with
playthings. How suddenly I am unanchored . . .

SUNGLASSES

They're my fashion finesse, hiding grief
with glamour. Wary to disguise the wet
red eyes with dark reflections, I wear
the same shades to beaches and burials,
holidays and hospices. My specs were made
to vanquish ultraviolet as if it were my
anguish. So once in a massive morgue
where death was quite a sight to see, I
appeared a tourist among those crowded
corpses, their glare never getting to me.

SUBSCRIBER AS SURVIVOR

For my luck, I look to *The Times*.
Print and pictures recount for me
disaster, misfortune, catastrophe,
unspeakable atrocity. I pour

a second cup of coffee. Collisions,
afflictions, murder, misery, poverty,
insanity. I pause to see what
the weather might be. Then I'm on

to so-and-so's obituary. But so-
and-so's no one I know. And some-
time we all have to go. So far, though,
not me. Any news breaking on TV?

REVISIONS, THEY

go with the territory, a ghostly gray terrain,
its brilliance near, so darkly insane. Mine
begin perhaps in water, that soothing certainty
of never surfacing. Or a poetic frozen fantasy,
deep snow, warm stupor, and letting go
at ten below. In a car, my motor's revved,
windows sealed, with a concrete wall ahead.
Eiderdown feels nice, with handfuls of pills,
snuggled in bed. Still, I'm far from dead.
My final decision is always another revision.
I need exercise. See a blind girl jumping rope.

THE WHITE EYELASH

Like Liquid Paper over a comma, never-
theless, I paused, the time to anticipate that
aberration as error, my mirror's mistake.

Years ago, an albino doe moved amid
the mascara forest of November, then
showed herself in a clearing of drifted

snow. Who would not blink at such a sight,
question the light? A hunter gauged that
startling white, an apparition haunting

his blood sport, as if an absence
of pigment might transport the target
to its fate. We see ourselves too late.

Ammunition accelerated her leaping
run. The wand of darkness had come.
In a blast or a blink, we succumb.

WELLERS BRIDGE ROAD

The trees told me nothing. They were too true
to tell. So I called them gray graphite lines
marking the pale sky well. The snow spoke
of silence, iced to an edge. STOP, a sign's

red contrivance and white letters read. Pausing
by a small failing farm, its pasture worn
like a ditch, I saw the auburn elegance
of an Irish setter bitch. Resolute, she held

her point, but still her neck swung; the tumor
weighting it was time in a pendulum. As I walked
just beyond that intersected field, another
sign, less vividly, read YIELD. There, like the ghost

of a species appearing from dusted ground,
a white squirrel foraged until in one ferocious
bound the setter set instinct free
and charged that pale vision up the nearest tree.

"NEVER ANY MORE INCEPTION THAN THIS"

I've been where the bougainvillaea descends
through the lattice roof and the mosaic fountain
splashes sunlight over lemon leaves. I've been
where the café is candlelit and crowded with every-
one looking interested and desirable. And I've been
in the library when words washed into brain
waves, rapturous as any turquoise tide shaping
a tropical shore. In rain, moonlight, and snow,
you've been there too. So I ask you, how do we
exit this dance floor gracefully? See the ghosts
gathering, wanting to cut in, changing the music.

SO NEAR AND YET

JUST BEFORE BED

Late one night walking across my lawn, I pitched
a large pinecone back at the trees and startled
some sleeping birds. Out of the branches they came
flapping, chirping with fright, then flew away
into the dark disquieted world, deranged as bats
at noon. There's nothing more to this, only the old
discomfort of wondering how to be acquainted with
the night without disturbing its peace. And where
does one go to nest again, or (perchance) to dream?

MY NEIGHBORS' HOUSE

One day in spring each year
their house will disappear
in overlapping new leaves
and the basketry branches weave.

Then some comfort seems gone
as if trees erased their lawn,
leaving me in a green sphere
without sensing someone near.

What's left is a slope worn tan
where the path between us began.
Later, when autumn descends,
their roof appears by season's end.

Yet winter is when I look more
toward their windows and their door
over fields and walls of stone
to see myself as less alone.

CUTTING THE BRAIDS

In memory of Tam Farrow

Such severity of scissors, my hands
had never known. Of all the ways,
this was the worst for a child to leave
her home. The blades severed
a thousand strands and then ten
thousand more as seconds sundered
years to come from all the years before.
To see her blind eyes closed, so cruel
an irony of sleep, made me hear more
sharply her mother's distress, her sisters'
weep. Nothing to do, but hold the braids
and open wide the door. As the stretcher
went out, I could not ignore an absence
of spirit that was not there before.

BREATH BY BREATH

Canary, the boy, winging his way
through the cave of their conflict,

testing its toxicity and attempting
to sing. Small birdsong starts as he

darts for light in an adult labyrinth
that opened with love and twisted

with fate. Flying into that darkness,
he tries to discern one side from

the other and gauge the distances
between. He wants to whistle past

the poisoned air, back to the life
they had back then, back there.

TOILE SKIRTS, LINEN SHEETS

Home from the ballet, he complained
the lead wasn't so good. Years ago
he'd seen the greatest, and now none

could compare. In bed, she lay listening
but seeing instead a young woman
stretching at the barre, feet calloused,

arms aching, her hopes grown heavy.
Both of them had tried, only to become
acceptable, but not quite his *Firebird*.

HOME STRETCH

Instead of outright, she affects being overheard.
Contemptuous sighs, incantations of anger,
murmurs murderous to the reconciliation of
mother and child, chilling in her isolation,

individuation, all so Electral, exaggerated
inflictions, adolescent establishing adult.
Oh, it is tiring, avoiding these minefields
of misunderstanding, assessing the short fuse,

its intent and impact. Sometimes I feel a stab,
heart saddening, stomach secreting acid.
Other times I admire a stranger's beauty,
her mane of hair, how hard she rides, loping

toward and away from love. Young goddess
in the saddle, sitting tall, contradicting all.

MEETING AT DIFFERENT CONVENTIONS IN THE SAME CITY

Arriving here took decades, luck, thousands
of dollars. And determination, however
unaware. But I stand here proudly
in my beige suit, bearing my briefcase,

loads of budgetary decisions, memos,
personnel problems, the underside of paper-
weights. An only child, an odd girl, I
never knew until this moment of moving

through a remote hotel lobby, how much of me
so-called equality has set free, all for one
historic instance of approving patriarchy.
How far I've come for such conventions. Ready

to see, however unexpectedly, one silver-
haired VP (aka Daddy), but more clearly, now,
to have him see me. After all, I know the muse
refuses measurable success, the cutting

edges of science and business. So when an old
executive perspective knows me in that split
second, born of our separate itineraries, I stand
apart his daughter and a part his own identity.

BELOW ZERO

It has been years since my father stood
in a field of snow. Today I wandered
over a hill so bright and white my eyes
could barely open against the glare, yet
I saw his bedsheets, smooth and drifting
over his large body grown small enough
to need mothering, weak enough to fear
the slightest cold. Though he lives amid
palm trees and steaming shopping centers,
he winters it out. Suffering this last season,
he finds no footprints to follow in such snow.

BEDSIDE

Holding his hand, the intravenous jabbed
and taped into his vein, she said, "Now
it's time to create vast funny thoughts,

things both cosmic and comical, for maybe
today you're going away on that huge journey.
A finale, God knows how it goes, but I don't

believe it's nothing. No, it's something.
Probably impossible to grasp, but still
with a hand, I bet, both masculine and

motherly. So let's reach over and see if
there's a way to turn the light out. I'll stay
while you think big, big as birth, no doubt."

CESAREAN

I wanted to come back another day.
A crazy pregnant panic insisted
on its way. "Hey, give me a minute."
He smiled. "I'm the one who's made to stay.

We'll do okay," he whispered in
conspiracy. "I'm your nurse. So don't you
worry. You know what to do. I'm Dave.
I'll hold you if you want me to." This huge

man masked in white gauze with glasses so
thick as to give one pause was offering
mercy to me. A laid-back angel of
absolute improbability, he took

my hand in that sterile room, painfully
bright, and began a calm anesthetic
dimming of the light. Spasms came from
below and quivers from above. Deep in

his arms, I knew the fear of oblivion,
each consequence of love. Cradled
by my stranger, my nerves slept at last; then
the surgeon's knife cut my future from my past.

Beyond the midriff curtain dividing
me came her cries so primal, so fully
free, that time split in two, half old/half new.
In my arms, she lay all pink and bloody

blue. Dave stood gazing down at her and me,
then wiping his glasses, said, "Dear God, she's
pretty." When his thick body lumbered
away, I could not find a word to say.

THE PRINCIPAL AND THE WEATHER

With her degrees behind her, she faces each wintry dawn
through the window's blur and decides about what is
never fully predicted. Between instinct and the Beaufort
scale, she weighs the flakes and estimates the ice
beyond the pane. Winter is what children do not know
even when they are hip-deep in snow: the consequences
of a blue sky turning to ash, the frost biting viciously,
the road so slick that their buses skid, as once they did.
For them, cancellations are simply little celebrations.
It takes years for all the lessons to be learned, and
always the principle "whether" is never fully discerned.

TEACHING BABY THE MOTHER TONGUE

Angel flesh, rose breath, hair spun
on spindles of celestial spiders.
(Do you know what I mean? The astral
arachnids who twist those itty-bitty
skeins?) Neonate nonsense, her exquisite
sensuality inspires a privacy of lamby-

pie lunacy of which one rarely tires.
I smile in this pinkness of thought
as gray matter grows rosy. (But who said
"Love those lil' toesies!"?) Articulation
eases into a cluck, a coo. Any good-natured
noise will do. So I allow each expression

to lose its teeth, for this milky style
is some relief. While world news shouts
of global pain, my tough-minded mouth
voices sweetness, no critique. She listens
as I speak. This perfect infant, all sixteen
pounds, loves my syntax and its silly sounds.

THE TERRIBLE THINGS PEOPLE DO

For my daughter, a local crime was the first shock.
Now, at ten, she asks about bombs with real fear.

Nazis have marched through her sleep, a nightmare
of hiding her friend Rebekah, whom they would kill.

The details of a torturer's table make her sick.
Good God, I miss those days when the only monster

was the Cookie Monster, when she mourned so hugely
one dead wren, and I encouraged her to smile again.

UNDER HOUSE ARREST

Now that my infant is almost an adult,
I will admit how one midnight I lifted
her tiny body out of the crib and carried it

far into a field. There I abandoned her
in the deep grass, alone with the blinking
fireflies, moth wings, owl cries, one wild

chance for fear or freedom. It seemed
a long time that I walked away, believing
in an intimacy of earth and innocence,

some Edenesque extreme so lost before
it was ever found. I had to give her those
orphaned hours under a cloud-swept moon,

in the pine-scented air. When I returned,
her eyes were wide, fixed on a galaxy,
her arms outstretched, not to embrace me

but reaching for that first mother, the one
beyond my absence who will always be, distant
as the heavens, instinctual as memory.

AT THE EXIT

In memory of C.D.B.
(1916–2001)

DRIVEWAY

Sullen, snide, sad, I was an adolescent
asked by my mother to open the garage door
while she waited behind the wheel. I walked
in front of the car and lifted the large handle.
As the door went up, I met my mother's eyes
through the windshield. When we went inside
the house she said, *You know that I just had
a chance to kill you.* I was silent for a week
or so. Ever after, when I did the door for her,
lifting to its roller track or lowering its weighty
closure, I thought of her foot pressing the pedal
and her angry heart braking for love and power.

MY AUNT'S LAST ANECDOTE

Against a tumble of flower baskets patterning
the wall, labyrinth of a childhood hall, the nurses
stood stiff as the points of their caps, each graduating

and fading into one tense shutter of time, dated
in gilt, 1909. Finding her mother's distant
stare and finger-counting nine months back,

she ran in tears to her aunt, realizing with dismay
what was relative, though not what to say. "Is Mama
mine? School ends in June; my birthday's too soon."

Upstairs, she was made to lie down, to sleep. Instead
she looked deep; disparities began to untwine
as if from the wallpaper's scheme of blue vine where

edges were showing through, dark stains of cracking glue.
Hours later, whispers moved into the stir of leaves
touching on the summerhouse eaves. She never forgot

that day, how picture and hook had been taken away.
Without a word, she was led to the door, then sent out
to play. Years later, drunk and dying, she would say,

"Now tell me if it's true. My sister was mother to me
and to you? Someone in this family knows the facts of
our maternal mystery, not that it matters anymore to me."

DRASTIC

Around our house, my mother had plenty of plastic: clear
runners over wall-to-wall white carpeting, polyurethane
flowers stuck into the garden, polystyrene fruits hanging
from a small tree, transparent boxes in all the cupboards,
garment bags enshrouding the clothes. Even a plastic cover
for the car. One day she feared another pregnancy, trans-
ferring her history to adolescent me. She put thick plastic
sheeting over my closet door. As her panic grew more drastic,
she had a locksmith attach huge bolts. Then she kept the key,
refusing to answer me. But I saw a crack of light. Plastic,
without plasticity, her mind I knew, was far from right.

THE UNDESERVING

The granddaughters are intelligent and pretty.
Her will affords them money in thirty years,
which she says is too soon. They need
to experience the depression, one of economy,
another of mind. *They have not worked hard
enough and do not save. Travel has spoiled them.
There's no place they haven't been.* The privilege
of their private schooling is met with public scolding.
She cannot tolerate their abundant experience
and gladness. It is an inequity she cannot forgive,
so she will not acknowledge their birthdays,
graduations, gifts, or even a joke. Life has denied
her plenty. Now the richness of her own blood piques.

STRIVING

Above all, my mother wanted me to be
popular, to be *well liked.* That was her hope,
her ambition for me. I was taught always to *avoid
unpleasant controversy.* So when I was nominated,
as a joke, to be high school prom princess, she
believed it was for real. She spent hours creating
slogans and posters for the coming election.
I dreaded the event and, worse, her regret at my
inevitable loss. My mother had been, as she liked
to admit, *something of a campus queen.* I laughed
once, saying, "How silly. What does that really mean?"
Now I'm sorry for those words. Youth is brief;
memories of triumph, however mythical, are sweet.

INTO THIN AIR

Flying over Chicago, she looked down from the plane
window and said, *I know I'll never see my city again.*
I didn't try to reassure her with a lie. Instead, secretly,
I began to cry, overwhelmed with jet speed and Godspeed,
clouds, cataracts, and all conclusive disappearances.

I mourned my own farewells, the ones I would never
know, my last look at a lilac, last apple bite, last café
at night. Yet what relief to be rid of the embracing adieu,
to drop, as I once did, a tennis racket, ring, and book,
without lament, never turning for even a second look.

MAKING NEW FRIENDS
IN THE NURSING HOME

Of course there is a cast of characters. Walter
with his heavy hands, a big noble man,
who sits with dignity awaiting his ultimate
appointment. The sisters, one a hyperbolic
hypochondriac, who greets everyone with
"Call 911! Oxygen is needed!" and the other
who is as unaffected as the air. "What a pair."
The nurse smiles as she explains to the new
visitor not to be alarmed into action. Camille
is the third floor thief. Ask the time and her wrist
will reveal six watches up her sleeve, the day's take.
Miami Vice is Miriam from Florida, leather-tan
and ready to bite, kick, or hit. Restrain her
hands and hear her plentiful profanity in a spray
of spit. "Mister Penn was at it again," the head RN
reports. "With a book over his lap. A classic!"

THE REC ROOM

The walls are decorated with large paper cutouts:
bunnies, pumpkins, turkeys, flags, hearts, et cetera,
according to the season. The social worker explains
these act as reminders of where we are in time,
helpers with our orientation. I nod in disbelief, wanting
to know where I am at this instant. When did I become
my mother's keeper? What is this place that seems
mysterious as Stonehenge on a dark day, surreal
as a performance by Cirque du Soleil? While Muzak
polkas play, the white-haired denizens stare at war
scenes raging on a silent TV. The imagery is circa 1943.

IN HER NEW DINING ROOM

"You get used to it"—the nurse shrugs—"though food fights
can be fierce." My mother refuses to eat with *the gargoyles,*
as she calls them. *Too many saliva straws have twisted
into their twisted mouths.* She can't face the obese moaner
whose mush is spooned in, caught on the chin, only
to begin . . . again. Then there's the fork tapper, who eats

with his fingers so his other hand can keep its constant beat.
One woman gargles her beverage between each bite, while
another keeps whimpering, "It's off. It's off. Overcooked.
Never right." No one need be afflicted with this company,
I vow, ready to arrange removal, find a proper place. Next day,
I've done it. The change is arranged. At the exit, my mother

screams. When her chair is even turned toward the door, she
shrieks, *Get me back, back, back in there! Just where do you
think you're going?* And so we stay, to enjoy an evening as easy
as applesauce. By Thursday, she has hurled a bowl of soup
plus two platters of peas. Everyone seems to have adjusted but
me. The nurse smiles. "It's normal here to feel certifiably crazy."

"HERE IS A PENCIL. PLEASE DRAW A CLOCK."

My circle is an oval that cannot find
its closure. The hands are minute arrows
pointing at the column of numbers,
one to ten, on the right, one to when.

I know this is not right. The clock tricked
me, ticked me. Doc Dickory. His mouse
mouth teeth click, tick. What does he know?
Braggadocio. I want to go. The point here

is missed. What clock? All poppycock.
Stop their talk. Strike one. Balk, walk.
Down he come. Leap into Lake Michigan!
Here's your specimen. I'll give you the time.

The doctor winds his paradigm. Late after-
noon. Inopportune to commit. So full
of shit. Claims the clock test is the best.
Yes! Tomorrow I was totally reassessed!

HER SKELETON

What went wrong sometime in the Twenties obsessed me.
I had to have the key to all those warped doors,
psychotically closed since childhood with a clarifying crime
on the other side. Once she said, *An incident awful and sexual
can damage an entire life.* Nothing more. Never more.
So I went to her sister, who later took a butcher knife
into the bathtub. I grew bolder, searched documents, spoke
to the sister-in-law in Seattle, played detective, biding my time.

Once death was definite, I asked again, direct as an arrow
into her ear, "Mother, please tell me what happened. Help me
to understand at last." A long pause. She calculated and
replied, *You know, you know what it was.* "No, I don't. Please
tell me." Then another pause. *That's enough. I'm going
to the bathroom,* she answered, wheeling away
down the bright corridor, taking a dark truth with her
triumphantly to the very end. The End.

SHE WAKES TO SAY

Merciless, the mornings. Stark, cruel corrections
of my dreams. Followed by the enforcement
of bodily functions. Then sprays, soaps, clothing
struggles, and smears of makeup. What can make up
for this? All the eighty years preceding are inadequate
consolation. Take away the nutritionist's tray. Resist
that physical therapist. Television has all the cadavers
transfixed. For a better fix, pass pills, close a coffin lid.
Get rid of any myth of ascension, comfort in the clouds.
I want pure oblivion. That's my goal. The friendly priest
appears scrubbed and ready for his surgery of the soul.

MRS. McB

An intelligent professional who agreed,
cheerfully, to be with my demented
mother for most of each day in the bedroom
and bathroom, accepting all the reality
of senility, tub and toilet, terrors and
trivialities, was Mrs. McB. She described
to me the value, even the vitality, of being
death's midwife, a tour guide through the end
of life. Accompanying her patients on their last
shopping trips to their last morphine drips,
Mrs. McB was an astute angel and authority,
who came daily to my mother's side and consoled
her with kindness and candor until she died.

LAST LAUGH

On what is called "a good day," meaning body and mind
are effectively medicated in adequate amounts, she wants
a tour of the corridors. So I wheel her down and around

only to realize, too late, a wrong turn. Moans of pain,
chilling cries, and hallucinatory salutations come out
of the "worst ward," where the patients are kept in

a circle of beds so the attendant can make repetitive
rounds in minutes, ringmaster tending his acts
under death's big top. As I try to move her away,

my mother hears it all, but she waves a careless hand
to stop me and says happily, *That's our little theater!*
Let's take in a show! As soon as they're through rehearsing!

TODAY IN HER WARD

Windows are upsetting the walls. Conspiracy
is in the curtains. At the corridor's end, scandal's
rampant. Call bells chime incessantly. Quantum
mechanics would come in handy here, for time
occupies several spaces simultaneously. We're all
in a different dimension, dementia. I'm asked if
it's frozen milk or melting snow and where does

the present go? Gift-wrapping and ribbon, or are we
talking *now?* Better than razor wire, synapses
snare, catch in the cranium, and show solitary
confinement on a comfy death row most inmates
don't want to know. But my mother's not ready
to quit, so we struggle, minute by week, hour by day,
trying to make some sense of it in our sad bewildered way.

COLLUSION

Hush signal.
A finger to the lips and eyes wide with consequence.
Today is all conspiracy.
The Kleenex box is not what it appears, bugged
like the water bottle, lightbulb, and towel bar.

Infiltration is everywhere.
Last night, she whispers, *the corridors were chaos.*
Impossible to authenticate the imposters.
Some came in uniforms like nurses.
Halloween costumes too! Now her hand signals start.

I try to talk about the weather, snow sparkling
at the window, but she clutches my arm, digs in
her nails, enraged by my outspoken risk.
Only hand signals allowed she states emphatically.
Hers are like an inept puppeteer.

I am an unsigned deaf-mute ignorant
of what her busy arthritic fingers say. Disgust soon
replaces paranoia, making for a more pleasant day.
She shouts, *I hope you get arrested for having everything*
your own way! And now, neither of us knows what to say.

COMING TO CLOSURE

Unscheduled evening visits were advised, a checkup
on institutional care. So I would arrive late at night
to see her asleep in clean sheets or earlier in the evening
to help her change into pajamas. Once I had to wait
in the rec room, so apt an abbreviation. Five elderly

residents were seated around a table, having their version
of a lively discussion. "Shut up," one would say. "No,
you shut up," said the next. Then another, "Don't you
tell him to shut up. You shut up." And "I told you
to shut up, just shut up. I mean shut up." "No, you're

the one who should shut up." "Yes, you shut up." After
about the tenth silencing, I left. Half an hour later, the same
conversation was louder; all at once they were yelling
at one another to shut up. They seemed to be enjoying
their repetitive venting. The shut-up shut-ins letting it all out.

VALIDATION THEORY

The theory is that not correcting builds their trust,
reduces anxiety, even restores dignity. So agree!
Allow Tuesday to be Saturday, concur that dead
friends are alive again, and Benny Goodman is

coming by between shows. Accept any wacky way
it goes. Sounds easy, but I'm wary of an edge
close to a precipice. One infraction can release
an avalanche of argument. There's trouble if I say,

"Stop, Mother, the bathroom is not that way." Or,
"The doctor isn't coming now. He came yesterday."
These realities incur her rage. Again, I learn the old
lesson: Obedience is best. I must withstand the test.

For years I avoided politics, religion, and sex. Still,
nothing I know is true unless Mother believes it too.

APHASIA TO AGNOSIA

The plastic kidney-shaped dish is for tooth brushing in bed.
She can rinse and spit in it. The pear-shaped bedpan is bigger.
All these adjectives are organic, but mean nothing now.
Even nouns can cause confusion. Objects, direct, indirect,
and actual, follow. Her toothbrush becomes a spoon.
The telephone is a hammer. Bowels move beyond
any propriety. Towels are waved as signal flags,
furiously not soliciting any right response. Clean clothes
are such a source of frustration that a single sleeve can open
into tears. Zippers are a calisthenics course, but buttons
suddenly become bonbons, resisting her eager bites.
So a piece of real chocolate is offered. Innocently,
she licks it and asks, *Did you address all my invitations?*

SEMIPRIVATE

From the curving metal ceiling track, small chains hang
suspending curtains, a mockery of privacy
that does not reach the floor or even meet at closure.
On the window side, a roommate crunches corn chips
and watches the jurisprudence of Judge Judy, a telly fave.
On the other side, against the wall, most definitely against

the wall is my mother. Dying. The months of her disease
are now reduced to hours and to this. Her morphine drips
behind the curtain, as Judy delivers another punch line,
"Don't tell me there's no contract. Where's the written
agreement?" Nothing agrees here. There is no contract.
Not even ice chips. In our cassette player is a tape,

Gregorian chants. But hours ago we lost this
iron-curtain war and we are in a crunch, so the last
judgment will be Judy's. The monks' celestial sound
will stay unheard, unwound. My mother will hear
how her contract was broken, lost before a commercial
break. Then those voices will continue on to lawn fertilizer,

deodorant, and dog food. Here I must ask you how
did the monsters of media collude with senility's roommate
and Doctor Death? I who would be reading Donne
am quite undone, left with my dying mother to suffer
through corn chips, morphine drips, diapers,
daytime TV, and this godforsaken absurdity.

MY MOTHER'S TALENT

Toward the end, she was an elliptical expert,
as imaginative and confounding as the best
minds straying all over the sense of things,

fragmentary, eccentric, and innovative,
an original voice, beyond every ordinary blurb.
Hers was an erasure of sequences, bedsheets

to bygones, water pitchers to world war,
deconstructing bandage and breeze,
she was a marvelous grab bag of maddening

metaphor, syntax whacked by synapse;
she found her genius at last: a poet (perhaps).

A LEGACY LIKE BETTY GRABLE'S

Nothing new in the nausea of the nursing home.
One word, say odors, will do. Drool makes two.

But this is about beauty and its unexpected
entrance into the repellent room of her dying.

When the bedsheet was lifted, her naked legs
were revealed, slender, smooth, and muscled,

as if she'd just kicked off those open-toed pumps
much prized in the Forties to find an eyebrow pencil

with which to draw a pseudo-nylon-stocking seam
down her naked calves. Underpinnings of her past

made her always unsure of any stance. Only her legs
held up, model-perfect on their runway to the morgue.

NO SERVICE, NO STONE.
CONSIDER ME ON MY OWN.

Those were her terms. Her ashes came back
packed in a cardboard box, the postage stamps
canceled as if certifying their date of death just

as hers had been. Where to scatter, she would
not say, so I too am "on my own," owing her
some ritual and return. My instruction is only

by intuition. She who has passed through earth
and fire must be delivered by air to water, our final
dissolution. We part in a wind over Lake Michigan.

CANTATA LYRICS

Music by David Carlson

*Commissioned by Glimmerglass Opera, New York
in Celebration of the 25th Anniversary Season*

*For chamber chorus, soloists,
nine solo strings, and harp*

CONSTELLATIONS

Through the invisible aura of air and space,
hear echoes of music, of infinite grace.
   A chorus sings through the night
with luminous voices as the heavens ignite Lyra and
Libra, Borealis bright, Cassiopeia, flickers
of light.
   Eternal beyond earth in a place
beyond air, the answers of angels are the pleasures
of prayer.
   Linking icons, beholding Aries or Orion,
visions of spirits, Lupus and lion, eagle and dove,
stargazing eyes stare above searching the dark
for an extreme reply, far past the moon and beyond
the sky.
   Hear the gathering song, celestial
and clear, swirling over clouds in the vast atmosphere,
worlds beyond words, in this music of spheres, sweeping
past earth and humanity's fears, exalting light
as darkness nears.
   Sing of the solstice, of Venus
and Mars, praising the cosmos, all planets and
stars, sing of the heavens, so lavishly ours.
   Saturnian splendor is the beauty
of rings, Cassini's division of immense imaginings.
   Beyond the father of Saturn, the god
of each sea, turns wingèd Mercury, and Hades' lord,
beckoning all to space unexplored.

Among Jovian giants are Galilean moons
with galaxies countless, endless, star-strewn.
Spirals and spectrums of pale blue
flame, continuous, evolving, as their masses became
waves of light, strings of air, eleven dimensions
that tear and repair.
Novae upon novae everywhere.
Hear shadows of sound, within mysterious
dark, drifting from our earth to the sidereal spark.
Space beyond years is of time unseen,
signs and dimensions, sublime as dreams.
Now sing a nocturne of quasars and stars,
praising our universe, its radiance bright, holding this moment
through rapturous night.
Darkening dust, diminishing light, lost
jewels of color drawn into white, comets fading faster
than sight, see Capella and Vega and Antares' fire.
Heaven is singing.
Here is its choir.

LIGHT FARE
AND ODDBALLS

NIGHT SHIFT: FRUIT COCKTAIL

Boiled until they slipped their skins,
the peaches slid down, then rolled
along the conveyor belt to the splitter

and on to me, *una gringa loca,* a pitter.
I grabbed, gouged, grabbed again. Hot
wafts of syrup made skin sticky, gluing

hair nets to hair, but unable to seal
earplugs from the din of six hundred
thousand jerking cans of tin. Truckloads

of green grapes tumbled through shoots
as cherries churned in vats of gruesome
dye. We women all wore white and stood

on the wet floor for eight hours or more,
ankles swelling over our orthopedic
shoes. Still, after decades of a better

life, I miss that moment when the dawn shafts
pierced steam, when *a certain slant of light*
gave drudgery such a celestial gleam.

FROM KITCHEN TO STUDIO

Studio to kitchen, back and forth,
the painter moves,
tongue to eye, spoon to brush,
palette knife to carving knife.

Rhubarb red mixes in her head
with rose madder.
She sees cadmium in carrots,
Windsor green in string beans.

Raw umber thickens in gravy.
Bananas ripen into aurora yellow.

Every egg is a temptation
for egg tempera; every oil
(olive, sesame, saffron) might
make a blended glaze.

Both easel and oven
bake her crusts to a burnt
sienna. Her blueberries' hue
is the purest Antwerp blue.

Eggplants and plums are indigo;
Chinese orange, shad roe.

On quimper or canvas,
she serves crème fraîche
in zinc white. Her lamb stew
is the brown of Vandyke.

Figs, as if by design, are both
rose doré and violet carmine.
All this mixing is true. She devours
colors and tastes them too, mixing

her paints with panache, adding
a drop of honey or a Tabasco splash.

BARBECUE

With stainless steel skewers, tapered tongs,
stick-resistant spatula, and basting brush in his hands,
in Bermuda shorts, golf shirt, apron, and flip-flops,
he stands anticipating the flicker
turning into flame, the ember glow,

the primitive reclaim of man: mastering meat and fire.
His cave rituals are made complete with charcoal,
hickory chips, and mesquite. Suburbanite, he
dons the oven mitt, ignites his kettle grill,
then relives a prehistoric salivary thrill.

UNFORTUNATE ICE CREAMS

Calamari Crunch
Cherry Cough Syrup Cream
Lima Bean Swirl
Chicken Liver Brittle
Anchovy Chip
Eggplant Excitemint
Strawberry Squid Surprise
Foie Gras Fudge Nut
Marshmallow Milk of Magnesia
Salami Spumoni
Butterscotch Sweet Meats
Pickled Cabbage Blast
Lime and Lard Nugget
Chocolate Osso Bucco
Eel and Oreo Chunk
Praline with Parakeet Feet

HER SPICE SHELF

Odd, this first date, left to
wait, a guest in her kitchen.
He stared at her spice shelf,
wondering at himself.

Allspice, arrowroot, and
cardamom, her bouquet
garni in earthenware:
each essence held him there.

Cinnamon, cassia,
chili peppers ranked
by "heat unit" degrees.
Recipes for alchemies?

Rosemary, saffron, sage,
sea salt, and savory,
his thoughts grew more heady.
She smiled. "Supper's ready."

Piquant and poignant, she
seasoned their chat,
then laughed: "How absurd!
I'm Ginger and you're Herb."

He relished each extract,
root, seed, leaf, and powder.
After her cream of tartar,
he knew no one smarter.

Through a grind of tarragon,
turmeric, thyme, and fate,
his mind kept on milling . . .
Her zest was too thrilling.

As if by star anise,
his future felt guided.
He saw his lost libido
deep in her jalapeño.

He said, "Something's changing.
My taste buds seem new."
She laughed. "You're a flirt.
Just eat your just dessert."

She'd made a concoction
of mocha cream, vanilla
bean, and a dash of mace.
Soon his heart began to race.

With the last creamy bite,
the moment seemed right.
It was his hungry dream
to kiss the chef de cuisine.

They were soon off to bed
and, days later, they wed.
But Herb still pays a price
for loving her and her spice.

Without any question,
he has indigestion.

A PLUM, A PEACH

The cut plum, tart amethyst, drips
juice from the wet jewel of its flesh
while the cut peach, freestone or cling,

is a mix, citrine cream and rose quartz,
blush and blossom. The crown of summer
is studded with sapphire berries and

garnet cherries. These gems born of
a branch are the orchard's affluence,
bounteous bijoux ripe for the bite.

MY INSATIABLE INNOCENT

Whenever I see them, any sort
of berries or cherries, all
black, red, blue, or blue-black,
I remember back to my child's
grin as she lifted her smeared
chin from a bowl of Bing cherries
and blueberries. Her red mouth
was a fright, something between
a Kewpie doll and Halloween; her
teeth were tinted blue, and her eyes
shone anew . . . with glut. Then
she spit a pit, just for the fun
of it, and smiled beyond dispute
in her own primitive pleasure,
a bacchanal of berries and cherries
before the inevitable aftermath
of stomach ache and bubble bath.

THE ELEGANCE OF ALBUMEN

Here this alchemy comes dear
unlike soapsuds or heads of
beer. All foams of egg always
beg artful exactitudes

of beating and heating as
each one seeks its defined
peaks, "danger points" to enable
a classic "eight-fold stable,"

that mass of bubbles made to
redouble without trouble.
The volume must puff like sea
spume with all the air it can

consume. Alas, there's nothing
blasé about a soufflé
or getting the elusive
hang of a perfect meringue.

No neophyte can master
the metamorphoses of
yolk or white. Fowl albumen
requires fairest acumen.

BLANK INSIDE

Remarkable that those cards, aisles of them,
piles of them, are entrusted to transmit
the elusive emotional messages
of so many. Sentiments and sympathies,
innumerable categories in which
to communicate, and they offer dispatch
in an envelope to match. Relationships
each with its own separate section: *Nephew,*
Secretary, Godchild, and there's no other
as big as *Mother. Christmas, Chanukah,* and
Kwanzaa are papered for celebration.
Birthday Masculine and *Anniversary*
Humorous meet broader designations like
Encouragement, Moving Away, and *Thinking*
of You. But best is *Blank Inside,* offering
an existential truth beyond description.
The whole mess could be recombined.
Imagine *Moving Away Encouragement* or
Humorous Thinking of Masculine You or
Blank Thinking Inside You. Or how about
Encouragement for Moving Away Mother?
When you care enough to send the very best.

"VESUVIUSATHOME@EARTHLINK.COM"

re: slant chat

em: plz cross lawn. ned better.
yr new one took off head top.
no fire warm. higg said no? fool.
lol at him. send letter to world.
dont stop. no auction. plz bring
carlo. gtg. flies buzzing. ttyl. sue

AN EMPTY SURFBOARD ON A FLAT SEA

Pomework: an exercise in occasional poetry
with the title assigned by *The Paris Review*

Dewey Weber or Hobie, it doesn't sing to me,
this Malibu imagery.
All cocoa buttery, I knew such things,
sunburned in bikini strings.
So bingo, no bitchin' allegory from me as
Sandra Dee. No beach-blanket
simile. Nothing Gidget cute in a wet suit,
just this surfer girl's testimony,
who in reality lived the movie
(while never feelin' groovy).
Still they can depress me, sand-castle
success and Funicello fantasy.
So old *Paris Review,* let me hang ten with you
and type what's true. I'll be the muse's slave
before I ever catch another wave or submit a poem
this depraved. Now go zinc your nose,
curl your toes, and publish prose.

THE OBLIGATION OF AVOIDANCE

The poem that you find
                    so aggravatingly incomprehensible
beginning with the octopus playing the pure piano
                                        off-key
with the word
playing
on the left margin   pure perfectly centered

                                        piano
several spaces down on the lower right

and "(OFF*key)"
in parenthethesis, with off capitalized in italics followed by
an asterisk referring
                    down to the word cephalopod,
bothers me a bit as well.

                            As it later alludes to
monoclonal antibodies, the Courthouse at Appomattox,
and then repeats the word sand in six places
where normal usage would make the word adjectival
in that extensive and supposedly essential alliterative lineup
of
        sand-stick, sand-stupor, sand-shock, sand-
        sensation, sand-situation, and sand-psycho
tries my patience.

And what the hell are all those hyphens for?
                                        Perhaps
the high priest of academe will come to our rescue
                with his keys so critical

for opening this cloistered door of metaphor?

                                                                    Or

is he part of a secret conspiracy? Is he hiding
the serial killer of accessibility?

                              Could be.

                              Beats me!

So what, pray tell, what does it mean

                              this poem

of salad greens

                              scattered over the subconscious

stream?
So many foreign words
and footnotes make folks want to

                              scream. Who

in good conscience writes such
things?

Is it because they cannot sing?

                              Turn their pages

away. That octopus doesn't know how to play or

                              what to say.

(Read his eye, touch his tentacles, but don't trust
        those encircling little suction cups.)

OPHIDIAN AFFECT

Both spinal and fluid, the movements are
undulating and minacious: sidewinding,
concertina, constriction, coil, and strike.

As a child, I ran home from my favorite
place to play, under willows by a stream,
where suddenly to my horror one came

weaving through the water. The only poison was
its presence, but that proved to be venomous
enough to my sanctuary. So serpents remain

with me: assailants ominous, though unlikely,
but molting in my mind, mythically provoking.
Cobra, boa, rattler, viper, Egyptian asp. . . .

IMITATING THE ANACONDA

Open wide. Wider. Unhinge your jaws. Wider.
Now swallow that piglet. Gulp again. Go a-
head. There it goes! Down to its tiny twisted
tail. Your gastric juices will dissolve skin, bone,
teeth, hair. (Feathers too!) Size can't stop you: feels great
to engorge and ingurgitate. There's nothing
quite like being fed an idea bigger
than your head; a thought that takes days to digest
will duly internalize to manifest.

LIGHTEN UP

they tell me, though being breezy has
never come easy. They want helium in
my cement mix. Confetti on the River
Styx. Balloons above a crucifix. Flowers
in a gravel pit. It doesn't fit. Joie de vie
just isn't me. My family's full of sorrow
and suicide. A hearse is not a Disney ride.
I clutch at conventionality, sensing near
insanity. Still, people tell me to lighten up,
after which I just tighten up. An overwound
watch with a loud alarm, ready for the next
hour's harm. As I see it, most enlightened
is most frightened. The merrier, the scarier.

NO LONGER HERE

TRUST

Trust that there is a tiger, muscular,
Tasmanian, and sly, which has never been
seen and never will be seen by any human
eye. Trust that thirty thousand sword-
fish will never near a ship, that far
from cameras or cars elephant herds live
long elephant lives. Believe that bees
by the billions find unidentified flowers
on unmapped marshes and mountains. Safe
in caves of contentment, bears sleep.
Through vast canyons, horses run while slowly
snakes stretch beyond their skins in the sun.
I must trust all this to be true, though
the few birds at my feeder watch the window
with small flutters of fear, so like my own.

ARRANGEMENTS FOR THE ENDANGERED

What crematorium will inter Hine's emerald
dragonfly, pour those iridescent green ashes
into a clear glass urn? What mortuary will lay
the Jamaican boa to rest in a thin narrow

elongated coffin? Or set on tufted satin
the Sumatran rhino before installing him in
the rhinoceros mausoleum? What "cause of death"
euphemism will pass for losing the pink fairy

armadillo or the African wild ass? Where is
the priest who will offer last rites to St. Vincent's
parrot or the rabbi to bury Koch's pitta?
What cortege can attend all twenty-three sea turtles,

eight different whales, fifteen extravagant pheasants?
Must eighteen monkeys fit into one simian crypt?
How to embalm all those butterflies? What eulogy
for the clawless Cameroon otter? Who will write

an obituary for the Alabama beach
mouse? Or offer the epitaphs for Bulmer's fruit bat,
the Tampico pearly mussel, Oahu tree snail,
every black jaguar, every last gorilla?

VEGAS

Addiction to the sound, coin in slot, what-
not, and then the merry electronic music
recalling calliopes with the metal clang
of change. Change! The unspoken promise
is change! As if to say, wealth, happiness,
and whores can all be yours! Amusing,
to observe the inestimable odds against
these vulgar aesthetics. How the perishing
republic shines, offering its casinos of hope
and indifference. The façade is supposed
to be such fun: tamed white tigers aflame,
fountains volcanic, pirate ships sinking
twice a day, as gondolas wind their watery
way through a shopping center's *second* floor.
But here in the desert, I feel myself a bore
beside Bellagio's artificial lake, worrying
about my country's indulgence, folly, and fate.

FILINGS

All over New York City, papers flew, feathers without
wings, landing with unintended import here, there, every-
where. Résumés floated unread in rivers, spreadsheets

littered schoolyards, theater tickets drifted onto rooftops,
paychecks dropped into chimneys, charred letters
scattered over streets. All faxes, bills, greeting cards,

accounts, and agendas were delivered through the air
to an unimagined elsewhere. How can a poem attempt
to follow such flights, reply to those random missives,

the grave communication of their inadvertent offerings?
Addressing anything is a poet's folly, igniting ink,
chasing the updraft, presuming the sparrow to be
a phoenix, ascending again from ashes with answers.

NEW YEAR'S DAY IN THE INNER HEBRIDES

Dreams and dismemberments, elf spots and sea locks, here
tales are told of knives stuck into doors, the inseparability
of screams and gales, and of a fairy marrying a favorite
son while his family sat bent over peat smoke in a stupor
of pipes and drones. Here, earth is named Skye; Isle

that is at once ancestral and alien, homey and hallucinatory.
Here, sheep stand among headstones but sleep on the road.
Here, boulders are split by the petal points of saxifrage,
ebb tides enter bottles, and visions consume centuries. Still,
nothing seems as strange as we, Americans in an Avis stuffed

with Shetland sweaters, shortbread, and suitcases. Our guide
book promises a glimpse of the Cuillins, and a Gaelic word,
though we have something else in mind. These are our days
in Dunvegan; we have come to dwell in the archetypal,
in grandeur grown ancient, amid vapors, and on an edge

with the elements. Things are exaggerated here. We are glad,
playing Ping-Pong in an aviary where lunge and volley touch
taxidermy, where gannets eye the game from their permanent
perch. After supper, an old fellow says, "Up here, you see,
it's all Celtic symbolism. The burns are bright, but the foam

is seething. I could show you glens that never respond to spring. I could feed you cloudberries and let you hear the hollow suck of waves sounding like your eager heart." On the Isle of Skye, extremes grow ordinary. Our host is a modern man made head of clan; his laugh is like music meeting calamity. His inheritance

is larger than life, for it is history. Between the oil portraits and the dungeon, he tells us that the castle's true keeper is now one with its ultimate invader: the tourist. "And they'll take anything," he adds, beside the worn balustrades protecting Boswell's bed. "Even Brussels sprouts; the gardener

couldn't keep them out." Time begins to dance a reel. A lone white croft disappears in the mist. Distances grow dim. A child comes in to tell of fox tracks in the frost. But no one follows. "Oh, God," the dark-eyed pianist sighs, "a castle is saying 'Home Sweet Home' to war and stone." Soon, we shiver and sing songs

about remembering. Past and present seem as one. We are the lords, just having fun. Inheritors of all this earth, this Skye, creatures of such an exhaustive search for crown or cross, by blood or brain, we stand the same under this framed tatter, "The Fairy Flag," Dunvegan's

standard, tapestry, and rag. Whether reverent, whimsical,
or superstitious, we kiss the pane of glass over these frayed
and bloodied threads, this window on the fading past.
On Skye, Dr. Johnson said, "What we came for is no longer
here." But for us, today is the first day of a new year.

THE HOUR BY FLOWER

The speckled bells of foxglove ring
a silent alarm,
an aromatic alert awakening hummingbirds
as if to insist it's time to needle nectar
for another day of digitalis.

The scent is subtle
but somehow shakes the trees
until those tiny iridescent torpors hidden
in the leaves become a frenzied blur of wings.

Who can believe such things?
At precisely four o'clock, the day's darkening,
another flower arches its pale fringed petals
into extreme accessibility and exudes a fragrance
so ambrosial and intense it stirs
the death's-head hawkmoth
from its shaded sleep.

Within seconds, the moth moves
from slumber to fixation,
for the evening air has delivered
an irresistible message
and the flower will have its way,
quite like a lover might say,
"Come now, I'm ready. Hurry. Don't delay."

CATCH

I keep secrets from myself.
Slow fish start to school
under the ice.

With a lure, you
try to catch one

though the silver slice
with moonstone sight
often escapes with the water.

Wet running or cold solid, we
have both to tackle. Perhaps

only death dives so deep
to come up certain, call
the catch. But cutting my stream

you are as sure-footed as it
is slippery. When hooking

a piece of the fish without
the flesh, you pull in a lace-
thin fin. In this ice fishing

I describe as deeply mine,
your barb kisses

my bite. We pull on
long strong lengths of line.

ENVISIONING

A century or so ago, an Italian landscape
architect designed these pebble paths to converge
before circling the fountain so that a man
and a woman might meet. She would approach

from the wide marble steps, he over the length
of lawn. Roses would offer their customary
allegory of petals and thorns, while box hedges
hinted enclosures of fate. Long before the man

and woman were born, their embrace had been
so schemed. Corinthian columns would stand
as subliminal assertions of ruin and rebirth
like the affect of steps leading into water.

How do I know all this is true? Last night I saw
the pair hurrying toward one another and I heard
her light laugh as he lifted her, a quick twirl,
before they vanished into the words of a poem.

FLORAL BLACKNESS

The Sleepwalker speaks: All visible wavelengths of light
deserted me. I was abandoned in a garden during a prolonged
absence of moonlight. At the base of certain tulip petals,
the blackness began. Ink rose out of the stems in ebony
ascensions. From the wall, the espaliered trees reached out,

tearing at my nightgown, while the poppies swirled the drug
of their charcoal centers into an opium delirium. Floral
blackness covered me, patching my eyes with the dense velvet
tatters of pansies, insisting that I know the colorless color
of deep oblivion, the imprint of night, the darkest enchantment.

STILL LIFE

Once so vivid this bouquet,
last flowers from our bed,
now touches the light with gray

as if denying each bright day
from which these colors bled.
Once so vivid this bouquet

now seeds the table in dismay
at how the days so swiftly fled.
Now touching the light with gray

these petals close against the day
and all the cold that lies ahead.
Once so vivid this bouquet,

like amaranths gone astray
or roses surrendering red,
now touches the light with gray.

Though fate and nature betray,
remember these blooms instead,
once so vivid. This bouquet
now touches the light with gray.

ESCAPEES

On the road not taken, a poem can be lost.
The mind wandered away on a pine-needle path
so the poem vanished in a stand of white birches

or on a paved street, got lost in the crowd. Maybe
it was tossed away like litter as the mind sped off
on a motorcycle with sirens screaming and police

lights flashing. (Perhaps a siren should scream when
a poem is lost.) Other poems tell some truth but too
slant, descending into a diagonal, disappearing

in a gravitational field, the geometry of a goner.
Some poems hear America singing, then stop listening
to the words. Soprano, baritone, and coloratura

combine to make sounds so sublime that the poet
puts down the pen. Meanwhile, that poem has left
Brooklyn for Butte and will expire in Anchorage.

The poet is flustered as if having lost door keys,
but of course it's no disaster. Losing a poem is an art,
not unlike losing one's mind or, worse, one's heart.